Dinosaurs

Pterodactyl

Daniel Nunn

www.raintreepublishers.co.uk
Visit our website to find out
more information about
Raintree books.

To order:

☎ Phone 0845 6044371

🖹 Fax +44 (0) 1865 312263

✉ Email myorders@raintreepublishers.co.uk

Customers from outside the UK please telephone +44 1865 312262

Raintree is an imprint of Capstone Global Library Limited,
a company incorporated in England and Wales having its
registered office at 7 Pilgrim Street, London, EC4V 6LB –
Registered company number: 6695582

Editorial: Daniel Nunn and Rachel Howells
Illustrations: James Field of Simon Girling and Associates
Design: Joanna Hinton-Malivoire
Picture research: Erica Newbery
Production: Duncan Gilbert

Printed in China

ISBN 978 0431 184494 (hardback)
11 10 09 08 07
10 9 8 7 6 5 4 3 2 1

ISBN 978 1 406 24414 4 (paperback)
12
10 9 8 7 6 5 4 3 2

British Library Cataloguing in Publication Data
Nunn, Daniel
Pterodactyl. – (Dinosaurs)

A full catalogue record for this book is available from the
British Library.

Acknowledgements
The publishers would like to thank the following for
permission to reproduce photographs: Alamy pp. 6 (Christian
Darkin), 20 (Chris Howes/Wild Places Photography), 22
(blickwinkel), 23 (Chris Howes/Wild Places Photography);
Corbis p. 7 (Zefa/ Sidney); Getty images p. 18 (Louie
Psihoyos); Masterfile p. 15 (Glen Wexler); Natural History
Museum p. 19; Superstock pp. 21 and 22 (age footstock).

Cover photograph of Pterodactyl reproduced with
permission of Masterfile/Glen Wexler.

Every effort has been made to contact copyright holders
of any material reproduced in this book. Any omissions will
be rectified in subsequent printings if notice is given to the
publishers.

Contents

The dinosaurs

Dinosaurs were reptiles.

Dinosaurs lived long ago.

Pterodactyls were reptiles.
Pterodactyls lived with dinosaurs.

Pterodactyls lived long ago.
Today there are no pterodactyls.

Pterodactyl

Iguanodon

Some dinosaurs were big.

But pterodactyls were small.

Pterodactyls had wings.

Pterodactyls could fly.

Pterodactyls moved slowly on land.

Pterodactyls were fast in the air.

Pterodactyls had big eyes.

Pterodactyls used their eyes to find food.

Pterodactyls ate insects.

Sometimes other reptiles
ate pterodactyls.

How do we know?

Scientists have found fossils
of pterodactyls.

Fossils are the bones of animals
which have turned to rock.

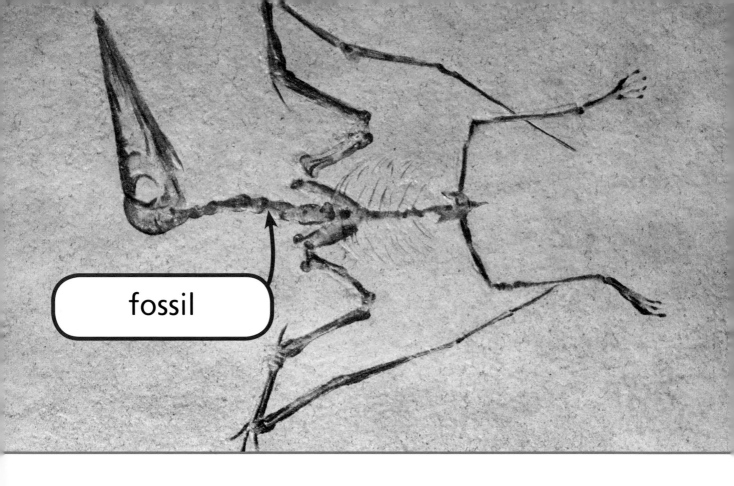

fossil

Fossils show us the outline
of the pterodactyl.

Fossils tell us what pterodactyls were like.

Fossil quiz

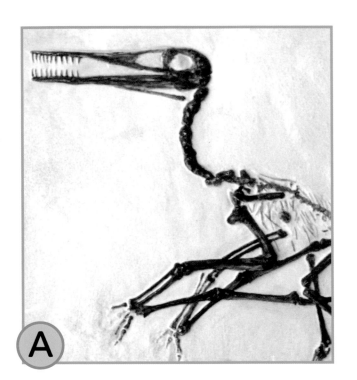

A

B

One of these fossils was a pterodactyl. Can you tell which one?

Picture glossary

 **dinosaur** a reptile who lived millions of years ago

 **fossil** part of a dead plant or animal that has become like hard rock

 **reptile** a cold-blooded animal

Answer to question on page 22
Fossil A was a pterodactyl.
Fossil B was Diplodocus.

Index

Note to Parents and Teachers
Before reading
Talk to the children about dinosaurs. Do they know the names of any dinosaurs? Have they ever heard of pterodactyls? These flying creatures were not dinosaurs but they lived at the same time as the dinosaurs.

After reading
- Making a pterodactyl mobile.
  Give the children collage material and card. Ask them to look at the pictures of the pterodactyl and to draw this onto card and cut it out. They should colour or use materials to cover the pterodactyl. Suspend the pterodactyls on a wire coat hanger from the ceiling.
- Read a dinosaur poem to the children e.g. *Dinosaur Poems* by John Foster, (Oxford University Press)
- Outside activity
  Tell the children to find a partner. One is to be a pterodactyl and the other an insect. Encourage the pterodactyls to move as if they are flying and to try to 'catch' their insect. When they have done this they should change roles.